With deep gratitude for your
work and ministry, and appreciation
for your continuing influence,

The Culture of God's Kingdom

Studies of the Beatitudes

Nick Wilson

WestBow
PRESS
A DIVISION OF THOMAS NELSON

WestBow Press books may be ordered through booksellers or by contacting:

WestBow Press
A Division of Thomas Nelson
1663 Liberty Drive
Bloomington, IN 47403
www.westbowpress.com
1-(866) 928-1240

ISBN: 978-1-4497-8278-8 (sc)
ISBN: 978-1-4497-8280-1 (e)
ISBN: 978-1-4497-8279-5 (hc)

Library of Congress Control Number: 2013901277

Printed in the United States of America

WestBow Press rev. date: 01/25/2013

Table of Contents

The Culture of the Kingdom

*Seeing the crowds, he went up on the mountain, and when
he sat down, his disciples came to him. And he opened his
mouth and taught them, saying: "Blessed are the poor in spirit,
for theirs is the kingdom of heaven. Blessed are those who
mourn, for they shall be comforted. Blessed are the meek, for
they shall inherit the earth. Blessed are those who hunger and
thirst for righteousness, for they shall be satisfied. Blessed are
the merciful, for they shall receive mercy. Blessed are the pure
in heart, for they shall see God. Blessed are the peacemakers,
for they shall be called sons of God. Blessed are those who are
persecuted for righteousness; sake, for theirs is the kingdom of
heaven. Blessed are you when others revile you and persecute
you and utter all kinds of evil against you falsely on my account.
Rejoice and be glad, for your reward is great in heaven,
for so they persecuted the prophets who were before you.*
-Matthew 5:1-12

Webster's Dictionary defines *culture* as, *the social and religious structures and intellectual and artistic manifestations that characterize a society.* Every society in history has had some type of a culture that defines it. This culture is comprised of their art, music, values, and the ways the people interact with one another.

The pervading culture of our day is considered post-modern. It is characterized by a distrust in many things that were considered truth in previous generations. It holds to the belief that truth is different for each person based on their specific circumstances and experiences. "Whatever feels good, do it," is the mentality of our modern world and we have even seen this philosophy creep into the church at times. This is a change from the Enlightenment culture of the late 17th and early 18th centuries. The culture of that day taught that science and fact could eventually explain everything that we see in the world around us.

Even in cultures that hold to a strong belief – whether it be in objective fact or relativism – there always seems to be some type of counter-culture within the larger society. A certain element of people are always willing to go against the popular culture of the time and live in a different way. Really, this is what Jesus was calling His people to do when He came onto the scene 2,000 years ago. the Sermon on the Mount in Matthew, chapters five through seven, is the manifesto of this counter-culture that goes against the values and norms of the society in which the people lived. This is the definition of what it means to be "called out" of the world, and the beatitudes listed in the first 12 verses define the character that God calls His people to display as they journey through this life. William Greathouse, in his book, *Wholeness In Christ,* tells us, "It is not too much to claim that the Sermon on the Mount is the essence of the Christian life."[1] Let's consider the characteristics of these traits that define life in God's kingdom.

"For the kingdom of God is not a matter of eating and drinking but of righteousness and peace and joy in the Holy Spirit."[2] This idea went completely against what the people of Israel expected in the days of Jesus. It goes against what many are expecting today. People had long sought a deliverer who would set up a political kingdom in this world and overcome those who have persecuted and imprisoned God's people for almost all of their history. When Jesus came into the world we were indeed invaded by a kingdom, but it was not the long expected kingdom. Instead, it was a kingdom that turned the values of the world upside down. The things that man pursued were considered of little value in this counter-culture established by Jesus Christ.

Man looks for riches and possessions, but Jesus came to turn the focus from those things back to the God who will provide all that we really need. God has taken the prideful, self-

---

1   W. Greathouse, *Wholeness In Christ* (Kansas City: Beacon Hill Press, 1998), p. 175

2   Romans 14:17

centered heart and turned it back toward Himself and His will through the power and the blood of Jesus Christ. He turned the unapologetic sinfulness of the human heart to mourning for those around us who are lost and dying with each passing day. He turned our human ideas and desires into a meekness in our soul that will listen and submit to the Holy Spirit. Our hunger and thirst are no longer for the evil that the world offers us which so often consumes us, but we now hunger and thirst for the very character of God Himself – righteousness. Jesus promised that we would be blessed for these very characteristics. As the holy character of God begins to define our lives we find that we are more fulfilled than we have ever been by any of the temporal things of the world. When man looked for a political kingdom to be set up by a revolutionary, Jesus brought what he really needed: a sacrifice that would purify his heart and make him a proper dwelling place for the Spirit of God.

These consuming qualities of the kingdom are not something we struggle through this life to attain by our sheer determination, but they are a character that is cultivated in our heart by the Holy Spirit as we surrender to God. His Spirit will instill these values in us, and allow us the blessing of God, as we submit to the rule of this invading kingdom. We so often try to attain these traits through dogged determination, and when that happens we miss the blessing of seeing God transform us through His work in our hearts. As Leonard

Ravenhill once wrote, "God does not want a partnership, He wants ownership."[3]

There is no guarantee that God will give us all the things we want, but Scripture promises us that He will bless us with the character we need. God will bless us and work in us to the extent that we are willing to submit our lives to Him. The only question is, how submissive are we willing to be? Francis Chan pointed out in his book, *Forgotten God,* "If all you want is a little Jesus to 'spiritualize' your life, a little extra God to keep you out of hell, you are missing out on the fullness of life you were created for."[4] A careful examination of Scripture leaves little doubt that the kingdom God promised us is a spiritual kingdom. It affects our hearts and minds more than it will affect most of our pocketbooks and bank accounts. God wants to rule over our souls, not simply our possessions – though that will be the result as our souls are placed in submission to Him.

The beatitudes are often looked at as a list of traits from which we choose. We pick a couple that we feel suit us best and don't spend much time thinking about the rest. When we view these characteristics in this way we could not be more inaccurate in our assessment. It is an assault on the nature of the kingdom, and the reign of Christ, to convince ourselves

3   L. Ravenhill, *Why Revival Tarries* (Minneapolis: Bethany House, 1987), p. 42

4   F. Chan, *Forgotten God* (Colorado Springs: David C. Cook, 2009), p. 122

that we can pick and choose what Scripture we will apply to our lives and what we will not. The kingdom is not about trying in our flesh to follow as many of God's commands as possible, or even doing "the best I can." The fact is, our best will never be good enough.

The kingdom is an issue of righteousness that comes from a heart turned toward God. The culture of the kingdom will never be the result of our half-hearted attempts to fulfill our obligation to God. This counter-culture is brought into being as the gospel of Jesus Christ transforms our lives, and it reveals the love of God to us in a way that changes our motives and desires. It turns us from our determination to accumulate the things of the world and focuses our attention toward the God who created us, pursued us, saved us, and sanctified us. This transformation is why the members of God's kingdom look different from the people of the world. God did not simply want to choose a few people who would acknowledge Him, but He desires fellowship with those who have been changed and transformed by His love.

Too often we forget about the Scriptural command to be transformed. We want the benefits of God's kingdom but refuse to become a part of the culture. The kingdom is something we acknowledge from a distance but never really experience. A.W. Tozer commented on this situation, "If the gospel does not change a man, transform him and take the evil out of him, then he does not have the gospel in power. The gospel is a transforming power; otherwise you have a name to live and you are dead."[5] Scripture teaches that if we are truly to be a part of God's kingdom we will be changed by His culture. The Apostle Paul told the Corinthian church, "Therefore, if anyone is in Christ, he is a new creation. The old has passed away; behold the new has come."[6] And to the Galatian church he said, "For neither circumcision counts for anything, nor uncircumcision, but a new creation."[7]

In our efforts to be blessed we forget that the idea of blessing necessitates some type of a change in our lives. To be blessed is to be changed, fulfilled, and brought into the joy of a relationship with God. To be *blessed* is to be one on whom God's blessing has been placed. The verb *bless* is a transitive verb in the English language. That means it has a changing effect on that object on which it works. So if God is blessing us it means that we are being changed and fulfilled. We are being given the joy of the Lord. We no longer need to search the world for something that will fulfill or complete us because God's blessing and love are at work in our lives and we are fulfilled by His love displayed through Christ in us. As the kingdom invades this world its culture will change our lives.

We must remember as we seek to see this culture work in our lives that there is little we can do to create it ourselves. Our own strength and will can never cultivate all of these

---

5   A. Tozer, *Reclaiming Christianity* (Ventura: Regal, 2009), p. 102

6   2 Corinthians 5:17

7   Galatians 5:16

characteristics; there will never be any program, process, or idea that will bring about this kingdom character. We must rely on God to provide what He has promised. God is our king, and He will establish the culture that He desires among His people. The characteristics listed in the beatitudes are produced by the Holy Spirit working in a submissive heart. We may look at some people in the world around us and believe they are "poor in spirit" or "meek," but sometimes these traits appear only on the surface to be the character taught by Jesus. They can never all come together in a single life apart from the work of the Spirit. These traits are a result of God overcoming what is natural to the world, and since they are opposite of what is natural they can never be produced by man no matter how determined he may be.

While we may be left powerless to effect change in the heart, God can humble the proudest hearts, and make the most wicked of men thirst for righteousness. We are born with the tendency to do what makes us feel good, and our culture promotes this idea. It is natural for us to look at the things around us and let our circumstances dictate the culture we create in our homes and lives. God has provided a culture for us that transcends all the cares of this physical world. He has invaded this earth with a culture that turns our attention from the things we can't control back to a God who loves us enough to provide for all of our needs and care for all of our hurts and difficulties. As our culture becomes one of faith, we begin to see God work in ways we never would have believed possible.

The things we struggled to do in our own power, the ministry we tried to promote through human ingenuity, the ideas we tried to perpetrate as heavenly vision pale in comparison to the uncanny power and might of God moving in the heart of His people. It is the kingdom culture that shows us the fullness of the supernatural power of God working among His people as they serve Him. The blessing we receive from living these traits is that we see God move in ways that others will never understand. Through this experience we are blessed.

We convince ourselves that God demands a change because He wants to deprive us of something, but nothing could be further from the truth. God calls us out of the culture of the world to a counter-culture where we can clearly see His power and grace on display through the lives of His people. We become vessels that carry this culture into the work place, or school, or to our families as God's kingdom invades this world. God's will is always to bless us, and as His culture is firmly established in our homes and relationships we will see His work in ways that we never imagined possible.

The blessing we experience is based on the establishment of a counter-culture created by God. As we live in this culture of submissiveness God's work will be done. How willing are we to live in such a culture of dependence on God? Will we allow the beatitudes taught by Christ to begin to work in our lives?

"To each of these saying belongs the message: the old aeon [age] is passing away. Through the proclamation of the gospel and through discipleship you are transferred into the new aeon of God."[8] Do we live in such a transformed culture? When you are at home what is the culture of your household? What culture goes with you to your social gatherings and work places? Jesus established a counter-culture when He invaded this world with God's kingdom. This culture is alive and well within the lives of God's servants today. Is this the culture in which you live?

---

8   Greathouse, *Wholeness in Christ*, p. 174

Blessed Are the Poor In Spirit

Blessed are the poor in spirit, for theirs is the kingdom of heaven.

-Matthew 5:3

In the beatitudes we see a way of life that invades the world through the redeeming work of Jesus Christ. They teach a culture that is contrary to that of the world, one that could be considered a counter-culture to any that society has ever known. The doctrine and lifestyle Jesus teaches takes the values of the world and turns them upside down. On the mountain that day, the Son of God revealed to His people a culture that transcends all the temporal subjects of this material world and turned their attention back to the spiritual things of God.

Jesus began this process by saying, "Blessed are the poor in spirit..." He had a very specific purpose and intent when He made this statement. Jesus was not saying – as some have taken Him to mean – that people are blessed simply for being materially poor. There are some who have found it a blessing to have fewer things tying them to the world in this life, but that is not what Jesus Christ was referring to.

He did not mean that we are to have "poor spirits." There are some who just aren't ever going to be happy about anything. They complain when things do not go so well, and then when life is good they complain even more because they have more to lose. They enjoy being angry and finding things to murmur about, forgetting that Scripture generally calls us to be content. This spirit can become contagious, and before we know it the poor spirit of a few has rubbed off on everyone. We end up with a whole group of people who are looking for things that just don't suit them so they can complain. This has become so common in the church that there is really no need to give examples. It seems at times like some are happier as their complaints become pettier. Maybe these people feel like they have been blessed with things to complain about, but nobody else feels blessed by it. This is certainly not the blessing of the kingdom of heaven.[9]

Jesus did not mean the "spiritually poor" either. These are the people who have forgotten what Jesus taught: "Do not lay up for yourselves treasures on earth, where moth and rust destroy and where thieves break in and steal, but lay up for yourselves treasures in heaven, where neither moth nor rust

---

9   M. Lloyd-Jones, *Studies in the Sermon On the Mount* (Grand Rapids: Wm. B. Eerdman's Publishing Company, 1987) – Jones addressed at great length the types of spiritual lives exhibited in the church in the 4th chapter.

destroys and where thieves do not break in and steal."[10] There are some whose spiritual lives are nonexistent; the only treasure they know is here on earth. They come to church week after week, sing the songs, and if pressed might even say a prayer. They will not acknowledge God when they leave the service on Sunday and some of them rarely acknowledge Him there. Their Bibles sit at home collecting dust on their bookshelves because, "I just know how God would want me to live." They live arrogant lifestyles and assume their minds are so much like God's that they don't really need His involvement in their lives. If there were ever a poor spiritual life it would be this one and, consequently, these are not the lives that receive the blessing of the kingdom of God.

When Jesus said, "Blessed are the poor in spirit," He was talking about those who stand humbly before their God, crying out for His mercy and love. He was referring to those who seek His will in all that they do and can't go on without Him; He spoke of the hearts that groan out in agony without the presence of a Holy God. These are the people God is seeking, and those whom He will bless. Isaiah 57:15 says, "For thus says the One who is high and lifted up, who inhabits eternity, whose name is Holy: 'I dwell in the high and holy place, and also with him who is of a contrite and lowly spirit...'" In this context, the word *poor* literally means, *a beggar*. God will bless those whose spirits cry out for His presence, those who beg to

---

10   Matthew 6:19, 20

see His power and are desperate to live within His will. It is these desperate souls who will experience the blessing of the kingdom of God.

In this verse Jesus refers to those who have come face to face with God and realize the gravity of such an experience; people who understand the power and the majesty of the One in whose presence they stand. Consider the response of those who have met God in a very real and intimate way throughout history:

Isaiah said, "Woe is me! For I am lost; for I am a man of unclean lips, and I dwell in the midst of a people of unclean lips; for my eyes have seen the King, the Lord of hosts!"[11]

The Apostle Paul said, "And falling on the ground he heard a voice from heaven…"[12]

The Apostle John said, "When I saw him, I fell at his feet as though dead…"[13]

When we are really in the presence of God we will be overcome with feelings of awe and humility. How can we not

---

11   Isaiah 6:5

12   Acts 9:4

13   Revelation 1:17

stand in wonder and amazement of the one who created the world around us and filled it with life? We walk with the One who created something that man – in spite of all his advancements – cannot create in a test tube, conjure with magic, or even explain. Martyn Lloyd-Jones wrote, "If one feels anything in the presence of God save utter poverty of spirit, it ultimately means that you have never faced Him."[14]

Our pride causes us to forget the greatness of God too often. It causes us to look away from the divine otherness that separates Him from, and raises Him above all of creation – including us. As long as we only measure ourselves against others in this world we can feel pretty good about the way we live and the things we value. We can feel alright about the culture we create in our homes and the culture we carry to the work place. Jesus is referring to the poor in spirit as men and women who have ceased to measure themselves against one another and the things of the world and have once again recaptured the command of scripture to, "be imitators of God."[15] They look to God as their standard and their measuring rod, and though they know we cannot literally be like God, they continue to seek His presence in their lives and submit to His Spirit in their hearts. They have consecrated their lives to His purposes and no longer seek the things of the world that will boost their ego and give them notoriety among man. They seek to let God be God so that they also may be what they were

14   Lloyd-Jones, *Studies in the Sermon on the Mount*, p. 45
15   Ephesians 5:1

created to be: His kingdom. William Greathouse tells us, "If to blur the distinction between Deity and ourselves is the root of all sin, to 'let God be God' is the root of all holiness."[16] The "poor in spirit" are those who are content with their purpose in Christ.

The reward of this poverty of spirit is the kingdom of God. The beatitudes tell us that this kingdom is theirs. When we cease to look within and begin looking to God to keep us and provide for us we find a blessedness that we cannot create for ourselves. There have been times that we have mistaken this within the holiness movement. Some have formed their lists of dos and don'ts that they claim lead to righteousness, but this is never the case. Righteousness is our total, unashamed, uninhibited reliance on God. That's why Jesus said, "Seek first the kingdom of God and His righteousness..."[17] When we seek His kingdom and His righteousness we are fulfilling our purpose. That passage in Matthew, chapter 6, tells us that God provides for all the animals and life that He created. They all fulfill their purpose, and He gives them what they need. Many times we find that we do not have what we need because we fail to fulfill the purpose for which God created us. If we will seek His kingdom and righteousness above wealth and riches we will find all that God desires for us. Oswald Chambers explains this says, "The bedrock of Jesus Christ's kingdom is

---

16 W. Greathouse, *Love Made Perfect*, (Kansas City: Beacon Hill, 1997), p. 26

17 Matthew 6:33

poverty, not possession; not decisions for Jesus Christ, but a sense of absolute futility, 'I cannot begin to do it.' Then, says Jesus, 'Blessed are you.'"[18]

Christianity does not value the things of the world, but the things of God. We do not seek the same things the world seeks, or live for the same things they live for. Too often the church of our day looks exactly like the world. We hold the same values and want the same things. We have convinced ourselves that there is no need whatsoever to look or act any different in our lifestyles. The world looks out for number one above all else, so that's how we live too. We will do whatever it takes to get ahead and achieve what we think we deserve. We accumulate as much as we can and build ourselves our own little kingdom in this world. But the kingdoms we build in our human pride will never compete with God's kingdom. His kingdom transcends all creation around us. If that kingdom is to be ours, we must swallow our pride and give up the building of these inferior little kingdoms in this life. John Wesley wrote, "One cannot but observe here, that Christianity begins just where heathen morality ends; poverty of spirit, conviction of sin, the renouncing of ourselves, the not having our own righteousness."[19] We build and build for lifetimes in our human pride forgetting the words of Jesus, "But God said to him,

18   O. Chambers, *Studies in the Sermon on the Mount* (Grand Rapids: Discovery House, 1995), p. 14

19   J. Wesley, *The Works of John Wesley Volume 5* (Grand Rapids: Baker Books, 2007), p. 256

'Fool! This night your soul is required of you, and the things you have prepared, whose will they be?' So is the one who lays up treasure for himself and is not rich toward God."[20]

God's kingdom blesses us with the sense of purpose that so many of us lack as we wander through this world looking for something more. How many people go through life today feeling like they are doing something that is just not fulfilling? Many are unhappy with their jobs, some feel like they have no direction, and others honestly believe they have no purpose in this world. There are people out there who have no idea what God created them to accomplish. They struggle from one day to the next trying to find something more but it never appears to them. It's because they are looking in the wrong places! God has provided a purpose for us, and He will bless those who are poor in spirit with that purpose. He will give them citizenship in an eternal kingdom that will last long after our life's work is over. This blessed purpose is where we find our sense of significance as we humble ourselves before God. Dennis Kinlaw explains, "Our sense of sacredness of human life comes from God, because He alone is holy. He alone gives worth to our lives. If we lose our relationship with Him, nothing has any value to us. But when we recognize that our personhood comes from Him, then we must treat our personhood as a divine gift with eternal significance."[21]

Do you see what we are dealing with here? Jesus is teaching

20   Luke 12:20, 21

21   D. Kinlaw, *We Live As Christ* (Greenwood: OMS International, 2001), p. 38

us that we are blessed, not by an action, but by a state of being. That's what the beatitudes are. When we become poor enough in spirit that God becomes the center of our attention we will live a life of blessedness in His kingdom. God empowers us when we come to the same realization as the Apostle Paul, that we have nothing in which to boast.[22] We become all that God wants us to be in and through our relationship with Jesus Christ! We allow ourselves to become so distracted by the philosophy and values of our culture that God never takes His rightful place. We worry about our self-esteem above everything else. We tell ourselves, "People need to think more highly of themselves and they will realize how much they can accomplish." We have been pulled into a belief that we must look within for fulfillment rather than looking to Heaven above. If we remember nothing else about being poor in spirit we must remember that it is always God who should consume us, never self. The Apostle Paul reminded the Philippian church, "Let nothing be done through selfish ambition or conceit, but in lowliness of mind let each esteem others better than himself."[23] The world tells us to esteem ourselves, but Scripture tells us to esteem others. Where are we going to stand? Where will the church and God's people stand today when the values of the world and the values of Scripture stand in direct opposition? James wrote, "For where jealousy and selfish ambition exist,

---

22   See Romans 2:23; Ephesians 2:8, 9
23   Philippians 2:3

there will be disorder and every vile practice."[24] But you may say, "self-esteem and selfish ambition are different issues." That is not so. When we instruct an entire society that you need to look out for yourself first, that you deserve whatever you want, and that nobody should ever tell you that something you believe is not right, what are we teaching? Is it any wonder that poverty of spirit is non-existent in our society today?

We can search the entirety of Scripture without finding a command from God to look within for answers to the issues we face in this life. But you will always find God teaching humility and submissiveness to His reign over us. It is through this submissive attitude that we are blessed. "All these things my hand has made, and so all these things came to be, declares the Lord. But this is the one to whom I will look: he who is humble and contrite in spirit and trembles at my word."[25] When we live for the world we have to keep up appearances. We have to get the house people expect us to have; we must conform everything to the standards of those around us because anything less does not create the necessary sense of pride. But when we are poor in spirit those worldly things no longer matter. We must live a life that puts us at peace with God, and it cannot make any difference what our neighbors and friends think of the small empires we have built for ourselves. Poverty of spirit places emphasis on what God finds important, and we

---

24   James 3:16
25   Isaiah 66:2

do not have to struggle to conform to the ever-changing whims of fickle humans.

How can God's kingdom possibly be the reward for maintaining a humble spirit? We understand that God will bless us, but what does this blessing mean? The truth is, God has always wanted to call His people out of the world to be His kingdom. Even from the beginning, He created a domain in the garden in Eden by placing man there as stewards under His rule. He has been building ever since. If you look at the 21st chapter of Revelation you find that Scripture begins with a garden and ends with a city. God is always building and creating.

There are two sides to this creative aspect of the gospel: a tearing down and a building up. Before God's kingdom can be established in our hearts, our human pride must be torn down. The idea that we don't need God must be dispelled if God will reign over our hearts. If we are to be fulfilled we must first be emptied so that God has a vessel to fill. This is why Paul reminded us, "We know that our old self was crucified with him…."[26] When we maintain our sense of pride and ego, esteeming ourselves above all else, God has no vessel to fill. He has nothing to carry His truth into the world, and no way to invade the pagan cultures of this sin-cursed earth with His gospel. Those who are poor in spirit have been sanctified and cleansed as they are filled with the truth of the gospel. This is

26   Romans 6:6

why Jesus prayed, "Sanctify them by your truth."[27] As God's truth fills the spaces that have been emptied of self, we are placed in the blessed position to see God work firsthand. His power is manifested in our lives and the lives of those around us. We see a power that we were created to carry, and purpose that we were designed to fulfill. Only when we come to the realization that we cannot find fulfillment and purpose on our own will we discover the opportunity to experience the blessing of God's presence in a deeper way.

This beatitude is the foundation to all the others, that's why it is first. All that we do as Christians is built on our reliance on God. He does not bless those who esteem themselves, but those who esteem Him, and others. When we tell ourselves how great we are, we have removed ourselves from a place of blessedness. We seek not to glorify ourselves, but for others to see how great God is through the testimonies of our lives. When we meditate on God's word and consider His strength there is nothing we cannot face. Can we say today, along with the Psalmist, "When I look at your heavens, the work of your fingers, the moon and the stars which you have set in place, what is man that you are mindful of him, and the son of man that you care for him?"[28]

The kingdom of heaven belongs to those who will bow themselves before its king; people who will live a life of

---

27   John 17:17

28   Psalm 8:3, 4

submissiveness to the will and the Word of God. Leonard Ravenhill wrote, "Yearly we use mountains of paper and rivers of ink reprinting dead men's brains, while the living Holy Ghost is seeking for men to trample underfoot their own learning, deflate their inflated ego, and confess that with all their seeing they are blind. Such men, at the price of brokenness and strong crying and tears, seek that they may be anointed with divine eyesalve, bought at the price of honest acknowledgment of poverty of soul."[29] If we are completely truthful, can we say the thought of God and His divine might really humble us? Does His self-sacrificing love that provided reconciliation give us the thrill and excitement that it used to?

"The way to become poor in spirit is to look at God. Read this Book about Him, read His law, look at what He expects from us, contemplate standing before Him."[30] If we are to inherit the kingdom, it will be when we catch a vision of a holy God who loves those who have never deserved it; a God who overwhelms our pride and sense of self-sufficiency. When we begin to see Him seated on His throne and are brought to our knees, as Isaiah, we can rightly cry out, "Blessed am I."

---

29 Ravenhill, *Why Revival Tarries*, p. 49

30 Lloyd-Jones, *Studies in the Sermon on the Mount*, p. 52

Blessed Are Those
Who Mourn

Blessed are those who mourn, for they shall be comforted.
-Matthew 5:4

The beatitudes outline for us the culture set in place by Jesus Christ at the establishment of the kingdom of God. These values go against those held by the world and show us a set of priorities that focuses on the spiritual part of our lives, the eternal aspects, rather than the things of this world. It almost seems paradoxical at times to say that we will be happy, or *blessed* when these traits begin to take hold of our lives through the power of the Holy Spirit. Maybe the most paradoxical of these statements is the second of the beatitudes, "Blessed are those who mourn, for they shall be comforted." What Jesus mean when he tells us to mourn? And how can we possibly be blessed by mourning?

The word *mourn* literally means, *the feeling or act of grieving.* There are things in our lives that cause us to grieve. The death of a loved one, or a difficult circumstance can sometimes be grievous events, but this is not the mourning to which Jesus referred as He preached to His disciples. Jesus is calling His people to grieve over the very things that grieve Him, and He pronounces a blessing on those who will mourn over the things that cause anguish in the heart of God.

Scripture tells us that evil grieves the heart of God. "The Lord saw that the wickedness of man was great in the earth, and that every intention of the thoughts of his heart was only evil continually. And the Lord was sorry that he had made man on the earth, and it grieved him to his heart."[31] God mourns over those who have turned their hearts from Him and set their sights on gaining for themselves all the things the world has to offer. Man has convinced himself that living a decent life will be enough to get him to heaven in spite of the great commandment given by Jesus to love God with all that we are. Setting our hearts on the things of the world is not "good sense," or "taking care of our families" or "doing what must be done," it is evil. There is no way around it and no excuse for it; turning our affections to anything less than God is simply evil. This evil grieves the heart of the God who loves us.

Disobedience to His commands (which comes from evil in our hearts) is another source of mourning for God. King Saul was an example of this. He had every advantage that anyone could have ever asked to possess. He was hand-picked by God

---

31   Genesis 6:5, 6

Himself to be the king of Israel; he had power, authority and remarkable wealth, but he did not have a heart to follow all the commands of God. The result of Saul's disobedience is not simply a slap on the wrist, but anguish, and regret in the heart of God. "And Samuel did not see Saul again until the day of his death, but Samuel grieved over Saul. And the Lord regretted that he had made Saul king over Israel." [32]

Some never make it as far as disobedience to what God has revealed because they simply do not believe. This unbelief, or denial of God, is a cause of His grief. Despite the efforts He makes to reveal Himself to man there are people who live in refusal to believe that there is anything greater than themselves. They contend that man is the highest form of evolution, and that someday the human race will evolve further into a higher form; life originated as part of a random series of events and whatever form of life happens to be the most powerful will survive (this belief is hard to reconcile with the fact that those who hold it also go to great lengths to protect animals that are dying off rather than adhering to their view of natural selection). This kind of unbelief causes great discontent with God, and the fullness of His power and love is never experienced because of this utter disbelief in His existence. Jesus went so far as to marvel at this attitude when He taught in His home town of Nazareth, "And he could do no mighty work there…and he marveled because of their unbelief."[33]

---

32 1 Samuel 15:35

33 Mark 6:5, 6

These attitudes and lifestyles were not exclusive to the time of Jesus. People still live the same way today. There are those who will turn their hearts from God to the things of the world, those who will completely disobey His Word, and still others who flatly deny His existence. If we make the claim to love God with all our hearts, realizing that these things cause Him to mourn, then how do we react to such grievous skepticism? When we look around the world and see such little value placed on human life, the dire consequences of the sin and evil that runs rampant through this world, and even the church – God's people – turning their back on Him how do we respond? Does it really grieve our hearts to see congregations cease all activity for the summer because people just don't have time for God right now? Whether we will admit it or not, we know it is happening and more frequently as the years pass. Does it cause any kind of anguish within our souls when even those who are supposed to be the church have abandoned the biblical teaching of creation in favor of an unproven theory of evolution?

Whether we realize it or not, we have ample reason to mourn. The sin that takes place in the world around us is almost more than the sensitive Christian heart can bear, and the willing acceptance of this sin by society is astounding. Never before has a society embraced the things that happen around us on a daily basis. Unborn children are sacrificed with the blessing of politicians who promise prosperity, wealth, and fairness. Thoughts of God are few and far between, and the world rages on at a torrid pace to hell. We conveniently forget that the sin of the world affects each life, including those of the children for whom many are responsible. We can try to the best of our abilities to ignore its consequences and explain why it isn't really so bad, but Scripture still says, "The wages of sin is death..."[34]

We seem to be predisposed to look at sin as an abstract issue. We acknowledge that it's there but never realize how it is affecting lives. Scripture tells us that sin holds people in bondage: "Truly, Truly, I say to you, everyone who commits sin is a slave to sin."[35] The sin that takes place today is keeping people from walking with God. It obscures their ability to see Him work and understand the reality of His love. It keeps them from understanding His word and holds them in place even as God tries to draw them near to Himself. Jesus calls us – even today – to mourn for the sin of the world.

We cannot stop by mourning for sin, however, we also mourn for the lost. Jesus offers us a blessing each time we shed a tear or travail in earnest prayer for those who do not know Him. We live in denial of the fact that so many in the world around us are headed for hell. Leonard Ravenhill wrote, "An unprecedented tidal wave of commandment-breaking, God-defying, soul-destroying iniquity sweeps the ocean of human affairs. Never before have men in the masses sold their souls

---

34   Romans 6:23
35   John 8:34

to the devil at such bargain prices."[36] Does this bother us at all? The fact that it is taking place around us is undeniable, but what will we do about it?

"You are of your father the devil, and your will is to do your father's desires..."[37] Some of our family, friends, and closest acquaintances belong to Satan, and nothing short of God's work through the mournful hearts of His people will claim their lost souls. These people are condemned to a lost world while we merrily go about our business. We will talk to them, play ball with them, and work with them. We participate in anything they want, but we so often refuse to intercede for them in earnest, mournful prayer. God may well speak of us as He spoke of the people of Israel through Isaiah, "He saw that there was no man, and wondered that there was no one to intercede..."[38]

Maybe the greatest source of mourning for God's people today should be closer to home than the sin of the world, or even the lost. It should quite possibly be for the church herself. The effect of the sin of the world has not been limited to the lives of those who do not know God, but its results are seen clearly within the church itself. We have been given a great responsibility that goes largely ignored in the busyness of our lives and the bustle of the world. Jesus commanded His people

---

36   Ravenhill, *Why Revival Tarries*, p. 93
37   John 8:44
38   Isaiah 59:16

to "go into all the world and make disciples,"[39] but the only reason we go into the world today seems to be to satisfy our own personal pleasures.

God has created potential within the church that greatly exceeds what we could ever imagine, but it goes largely untapped because we are enamored with the distractions of the world. When God's people came together in Scripture the ground was shaken and mighty works were done. Today we are lucky to get God's people together. Congregations all but shut down for the summer because "we are just too busy" with sports, hobbies, and vacations among many other things. Jesus promised us the "keys to the kingdom of heaven"[40] and great power to do mighty works through the Holy Spirit, but we would much rather catch a big fish, play a good round of golf, or any number of other things. If we are going to mourn for anything today, let it be about the impotence of the church in this sinful world. God has placed us here to spread a culture that originated in heaven, but we do the best we can to bring the culture of the world back to the church.

If we look around the world and honestly assess the sinful things that are taking place we have to admit that a great deal of this is our own fault. When the world needed people to take a stand against sinful things we joyfully joined them in what they were doing. When they needed direction from God Himself we ignored His word and told them that we would go

39   Matthew 28:19

40   Matthew 16:19

along with whatever they wanted to do as long as they didn't bother us. Martyn Lloyd-Jones wrote, "If we have no sense of responsibility for the condition of humanity at this moment, then there is only one thing to say – if we are Christians at all we are very poor ones. If we are only concerned about ourselves and our own happiness, and if the moral condition of society and the tragedy of the whole world does not grieve us, if we are not disturbed at the way in which men blaspheme the name of God and all the arrogance of sin – well, what can be said about us?"[41] If the world is to know the power of God and experience a fresh work of His Spirit it will be through the mournful hearts of Christians.

When we feel a grief over sin, and understand in our poverty of spirit that we have no innate power or ability to fix the evil of this world, something happens within our hearts that turns attention from our own frailty to the limitless power of our Holy God. The facts we know about His character are brought forth from our memories and we come to the realization that God must judge sin. The character of God does not change, and while God loves us, He must also judge sin if the Scripture holds true, "For I the Lord do not change..."[42] Through the fervent intercession of His church the judgment of God on those who are disobedient and live in disbelief can be averted.

---

41   Lloyd-Jones, *Joy Unspeakable* (Wheaton: Harold Shaw Publishers, 1984), p. 16

42   Malachi 3:6

They will be given opportunities to return to God through the prayers and outcry of those who would stand before God as mediators.

When our grief-stricken hearts are humbled to mourning God will release our friends and loved ones from the bondage of sin that holds their hearts in chains. God can provide those around us with opportunity for repentance when we become saddened by the sin that curses their lives and infects their hearts and souls. It is true that an individual who refuses the grace of God will not be saved, but Christians, through the outcry of mournful hearts can bring about the opportunity for their salvation. However it takes our soul-anguish to bring about these cries for the power of God. Tozer reminds us, "When the Lord releases a man, he is free; and until he is released, you cannot sing him free, you cannot pound him free, you cannot preach him free and you cannot get him free any way known to mortal man. Yet the Church spends millions of dollars every year putting on religious stuff in order to try to get people free. One simple act of the Holy Spirit will free a man; free him forever and turn him loose. And you can go to God and get bold about it."[43]

The church that mourns ushers the power of heaven and the culture of God's kingdom into a darkened, sinful world. When our hearts surrender to God's will His power will begin to move through those humbled spirits that have become His

---

43   Tozer, *Reclaiming Christianity,* p. 28

vessels. "The Lord is with you while you are with him. If you seek him, he will be found by you, but if you forsake him, he will forsake you."[44] When we have placed ourselves in a position where all we want is to see the power of God invade this world we will see Him move. "You will seek me and find me, when you seek me with all your heart."[45] Scripture promises us that God's Spirit will move when we set our hearts to find Him in the midst of all the turmoil and strife of this world.

As unlikely as it may seem, our mournful spirit does not cause us to walk through this life with no hope. Jesus promised that those who mourn are blessed and that they will be comforted. As we see our families and friends drawn to our Lord while living this great counter-culture we find comfort in knowing that the cry of our hearts has been answered by the hand of God. His work becomes evident in the world around us, and we experience first-hand the saving power of Jesus Christ as it works directly through us in the lives of those who so desperately need Him.

As we see God work in this way our mourning gives reason for great joy. It gives us a hope of something greater than we have yet seen. God told us through Jeremiah, "Then shall the young women rejoice in the dance, and the young men and the old shall be merry. I will turn their mourning into joy; I

44   2 Chronicles 15:2

45   Jeremiah 29:13

will comfort them, and give them gladness for sorrow."[46] As we see God's might working in the world to overcome the sinful values of this society, we can cry out with the Psalmist, "You have turned for me my mourning into dancing; you have loosed my sackcloth and clothed me with gladness…"[47] If we will humble ourselves, and turn our attention to God as we lament the state of the world, and even the church today, we will find great joy as we see the work of God take place in our lives and the communities surrounding us.

One of the greatest weaknesses in the church today is a defective, deficient understanding of sin. We no longer understand that "the wages of sin is death." The church that models the culture of the kingdom weeps and mourns for such a society, for those who have been lured by its relativistic attraction, and for the church that has compromised to meet its standards. We rightly grieve and mourn today, not over worldly things, but over those things which grieve the heart of God. When is the last time we grieved over sin? Or over the world around us? Or for the state of the church?

46   Jeremiah 31:13
47   Psalm 30:11

Blessed Are the Meek

Blessed are the meek, for they shall inherit the earth.
-Matthew 5:5

W hen I was in high school I decided to spend the beginning of one summer umpiring Little League baseball games to earn extra money. I did that for a few years and decided to do something more substantial, so I got a certification to umpire high school baseball games. For a few years I took part in those games, and during that time something stood out that I had never noticed when I played baseball during my childhood.

When a game begins both teams have a hope of winning. The players have received instruction from their coach during practices and they take the field to apply the fundamental principles of baseball that they have learned. They believe that as long as they apply what they have been taught by their coach, and do not deviate from the plan, there is little that can keep them from victory.

But we learn early in life that sometimes things don't go

the way we had planned. A player could make a mistake, or something unexpected might happen that takes the focus from the plan. Many times failure to execute the plan can be catastrophic for the team. The players are not sure what to do and it becomes even more important for them to listen for the instruction of their coach; however, when things get bad enough that the plan changes, players begin to hear the advice of people besides their coach. The score becomes lopsided and one by one the parents in the bleachers begin to call out instructions to the team. They all seem to know what needs to happen and what each player should do, and very few are shy about sharing that advice publicly.[48] As the situation deteriorates, the only hope of the team is to listen through the voices that call out to them for the one voice that will bring them together – the voice of their coach. That is the one voice that will offer consistent counsel and bring the team together, giving them the hope of victory.

Our charge to carry the culture of God's kingdom into the world around us is similar to those baseball games in some ways. We have been called by God for a specific purpose, and to carry out a plan. God has taught us through His Word what we need to know to live within the culture of His kingdom. As we live within God's counsel that we receive in His revelation, we are confronted by voices that call out for our attention. People all around us know what we need to do, and how we need to

---

48   I know Christians would never do this, and firmly believe that you have never publicly interfered with the coach of your children. We consider this solely for the sake of illustrating the point.

live. Some know how we should handle our finances and what we should do with our free time.

Among the voices that cry out for the attention of the church is the voice of current trends.[49] The things of this life go through cycles; some things become desirable and then their popularity fades. We see this in clothing, music, and many other parts of popular culture, and the church is not immune to this. For years the church has tried to incorporate popular elements of culture into our worship and the overall work of God. The purity to which Scripture has called us is compromised when we begin to allow the culture of the world to dictate the culture of the kingdom of God. We go through phases of using certain fads and programs, and then those pass and something new comes along, but this should not be. We cannot allow the world to change the church; it is the call of the church to change the culture and the values of the world around us through the power of God. But the voice of trends calls out to us nonetheless.

The church also contends with voices that originate a little closer to us. Tradition is often allowed to control the work of God's church. While at times it helps to focus us on the foundation we have been given, it also has the potential to distract us from that very foundation. We have, in some instances, been guilty of forgetting the call to invade this world on behalf of

---

49   B. Konstantopoulos, *The Virtues of a Healthy Church* (Prestonburg: Reformation Publishers, 2011) – Bill Konstantopoulos addresses the voices that call out for the attention of the church today. In this discussion he addresses the voice of the trends, the voice of tradition, as well as other issues. The voices addressed in this chapter are based on this book.

God's kingdom as we endeavor to maintain the traditions we have put in place. Our identity becomes so closely associated with certain customs that it becomes almost impossible to follow the guidance of God's Word and Spirit. Throughout the history of the church there have been times when Jesus could have said of us as He did of the Pharisees, "in vain do they worship me, teaching as doctrines the commandments of men. You leave the commandment of God and hold to the tradition of men."[50]

In addition to trends and tradition, values of the world call out to the people of God. The culture of the world always takes our attention away from God and points it to the riches that the world values. The world continually tries to catch our gaze with things that it tells us we must have, and too often we allow ourselves to be convinced that we need what it has to offer. We get caught up in seeking wealth and possessions and it becomes impossible to carry out the call that God has given us to create a different culture in our lives.

These voices are always calling us and vying for our attention. But as these voices cry out to us there is one – that still, small voice that cried out to Elijah so many years ago – that will give us the direction we need to live the lives to which God has called us. The voice of God calls out among all the voices of the world, pleading for us to sit back in a spirit of humility and meekness to listen for His direction. It transcends the culture, the trends, and even

---

50   Mark 7:7, 8

the tradition that we have put in place as God's voice draws us to something more. It calls us out of the world into His marvelous light.[51]

The church today stands in need of those who will be meek enough to listen for this voice as it stands in stark contrast, and direct opposition, to the culture of the world. God uses teachers who are not afraid to stand up for His Word and who will be sensitive to the gentle whisper of His Spirit. As unpopular as it may be to proclaim the whole counsel of God, it must be done. But the necessity of our day is men and women who will listen for this counsel, people who are not afraid to tackle the depth of Scripture and seek out all that God has to offer us. God called His people to this character of meekness long ago when he said, "Therefore, you shepherds, hear the word of the Lord…."[52] If the Word is ever to move in power today we must be willing to listen to the prophecy of the Word and proclaim what God reveals to us through the power of His Spirit. God speaks to men and women who will say along with A.W. Tozer, "I do not know what the future holds. But I know one thing: Rather than betray the sheep of God, rather than lie to them and deceive them and keep them agitated and stirred up with all kinds of popular topics; rather than take my material from *Time* magazine, I'll preach the Word to empty seats and sigh and cry for the abomination that is in the earth."[53]

---

51   1 Peter 2:9

52   Ezekiel 34:7

53   Tozer, *Reclaiming Christianity,* p. 143

We live in a day when the voices of the world have become so strong that they drown out the voice of God. When we want to see a renewal of God's power we invent a program in an attempt to bribe God into displaying it. We get together and talk about what we think we should do, take the best of our ideas, and ask God to bless them. Never in this process do we listen for the voice of God as He speaks His will to us, or search Scripture for direction. If we want to see the Word move in power we must be meek enough to listen for God's direction as to how to carry out His will. Why is that so hard for us to do? It only makes sense that if we are carrying the culture of His kingdom we should do it His way, but sometimes we just can't seem to recognize that. We might be humble and spend our time mourning for the state of the world, but unless we are willing to be meek enough to listen for God's direction those things will not do much good. God leads those who will listen to His voice.

Too many Christian lives – and the work of too many congregations – are trial and error. We just do what we think we should do and if that doesn't work we will try something else. We convince ourselves that it's alright to live that way because it's risky business to do God's work. Where do we see that in Scripture? When was it ever a risk to follow the will of God? We may face persecution or trials, but God has never done anything to give us the impression that He will not sustain us if we will follow His will.

The meek are never alone. They spend their lives listening for

God's direction as they serve Him and do His work, and they are willing to test the Word that God's Spirit speaks to them. We have conditioned ourselves not to test the promises of God because Jesus said that "we should never test God."[54] That has become our excuse for disobedience. Jesus said that when He was tempted, by Satan, to do something that would bring glory to Himself rather than God. Scripture teaches us that God's promises are for us and we can test the power God has promised to us. The entire ministry of Jesus was such a test. Everything the disciples did in His name was such a test. Scripture even tells us, "Bring the full tithe into the storehouse, that there may be food in my house. And thereby put me to the test, says the Lord of hosts, if I will not open the windows of heaven for you and pour down for you a blessing until there is no more need."[55]

The meek are familiar enough with God's voice that they will trust Him as He speaks to them. Those who are not gentle and lowly enough to listen for Him will never be familiar enough with the shepherd's voice to hear when He calls out from among those overwhelming voices of the world.

The meek have the power to walk through this life under the direction of God's Word, and they also possess the discipline to overcome temptation. Despite what we so often think, meekness does not make us a doormat. It is not weakness. Kenneth Jones wrote,

---

54 Matthew 4:7

55 Malachi 3:10

"The meek person does not fight back at persecutors, not because he or she is weak-willed, but because he or she is so sure of his or her rightness before God that he or she is willing to be mistreated since he or she knows that God and right will win in the end."[56]

Moses faced opposition from his own family when Aaron and Miriam opposed him.[57] He could have had them excommunicated or even killed, but this man was so in tune with the will of God, and had listened to the voice that called out to him to such an extent that he did not need to respond in a heavy-handed manner. Numbers 12:3 tells us, "Now the man Moses was very meek, more than all people who were on the face of the earth." He did not show weakness by being meek, but a resolve to follow God's voice in any circumstance.

This power came from a devout faith in the voice of the One who spoke the Word to him. He knew that he could trust the voice of God and when a question or a difficulty arose, Moses knew enough to listen for the voice that would guide him. He did not form an exploratory committee to research the sociological effects of the situation. He listened for God. It is not our ingenuity or determination that will deliver the culture of the Kingdom into the world. It is the Word of God working

---

56   K. Jones, *Commitment to Holiness* (Anderson: Warner Press, 1985), p. 174
57   Numbers 12

in and through our lives. This will bring the counter-culture of God to those who so desperately need it.

Scripture tells us that meek shall "inherit the earth." They are heirs of what rightfully belongs to God. They need not create a revolution or raise up a great army, but usher the culture of heaven to earth by the power of God at work within them. They are those through whom God answers the prayer "Thy Kingdom come, Thy will be done in earth as it is in heaven."[58]

Those who will experience God's power firsthand as He invades the earth with this heavenly culture are the meek. Men and women who will not charge ahead without direction, but understand what it means to "wait upon the Lord."[59] God has given such people a call to represent Him in this world as priests. "But you are a chosen race, a royal priesthood, a holy nation, a people for his own possession..."[60] They reflect His image in the place that He created to be His domain, or kingdom. Look at the rest of the words of the Apostle Peter in this verse, "But you are a chosen race, a royal priesthood...that you may proclaim the excellencies of him who called you out of darkness into his marvelous light."

The meek are the ambassadors of God's grace and mercy. They are stewards of the Word which He has spoken to, and through them. If we are to see God's work in the world today, it will be

---

58   Matthew 6:10 (KJV)

59   Isaiah 40:31

60   1 Peter 2:9

when we take the time to listen to His Word as it is revealed to us by His Holy Spirit. In a day when programs and ideas dominate the church, we would do well to remember that it is the meek who will inherit the earth. Maybe today we need a moratorium; not on offshore oil drilling as those put in place by governments, but on programs and activities in God's church. Maybe we need to spend some time meekly listening for the voice of God. We are called to carry His Word into the world, but when was the last time we honestly, earnestly listened for His voice? The church needs nothing more today than the voice of God.

According to Leonard Ravenhill, "If the church today had as many agonizers as she has advisers we would have revival in a year!"[61] Among all the voices of the world there is one that calls out to us and speaks of a future and a hope. He cries out as Jeremiah did so many years ago, "I know the plans I have for you...to give you a future and a hope." He has promised a blessed inheritance to those who will heed His voice. He has revealed Himself in His Word and speaks to the church today through His Spirit. Will we listen? God will bring His culture into the world today through those who are meek. Will He find such a person in you?

---

61   Ravenhill, *Why Revival Tarries*, p. 40

Blessed Are Those Who Hunger and Thirst...

Blessed are those who hunger and thirst for righteousness,
for they shall be satisfied.
-Matthew 5:6

A ppetite is a natural function of the body. If our bodies are to work properly, they require some type of nourishment. We get that through the things we eat and drink. Our digestive system reduces the things we ingest into nutrients that will fuel our bodies to carry out the things we do. It separates out the things that will provide us with the nourishment that is necessary to perform our activities and expels the rest. Some types of food and drinks provide us a great deal of sustenance while others are comprised of things that do not have such a positive effect on our bodies. Some people are very cautious about what they eat and drink, and the ways that those things will nurture them; while others don't put much thought into it. They allow their appetite to drive them to eat whatever they like. It is not my purpose to make a judgment one way or another on how we react to our appetite, but simply to point out that it is a reality. No matter who we are, or what we do, we all know the feelings of hunger and thirst. They are a part of every life, and every day of each life.

Appetite is the body's way of calling for the nourishment that is imperative to sustain life. When we get hungry or thirsty enough, our body begins to tell us. I'm sure we have all been seated next to someone at a movie theater or worship service and heard their stomach start to rumble. Maybe it has even happened to you. When this takes place you are being informed by your stomach that it is becoming a necessity for your body to take in vitamins and minerals and other things that are necessary to your well-being.

Usually when we begin to get hungry or thirsty the first thing we do is look for something to eat or drink. We go to our refrigerator, or, if we are away from home, try to find the nearest place that can provide these things for us. If our body is going to feel at peace, or fulfilled, we need them.

We go to great lengths to please our body and its appetites. We will go looking for specific kinds of food we think we want, or the things that we like best. Some will spend a great deal of time and energy finding the things that their body will use most efficiently as they do the activities that they enjoy.

We give great consideration to our bodies, but have you ever wondered what would happen if we went to such boundless lengths to satisfy our spirit? We give our bodies fulfillment so that we grow and live healthy lives, but are there any similarities to our spiritual life? What might we come to learn from this hunger and thirst that has been built within us, this desire to get what is necessary to survive and continue on? There is more to appetite than simply eating when we are hungry, or drinking when we are thirsty. Consider how these desires for what we need might impact our spiritual life.

As appetite is a natural function of our body, it is just as natural to the spirit. Our spirit must be nourished just like the body, but the things that satisfy our body can never satisfy the spirit. The food we eat can never bring a peace within our soul. The water that we drink will never diminish the thirst that has been built within us for fellowship with something, or someone, greater than ourselves. Adam Clarke wrote, "As the body has its natural appetites of hunger and thirst for the food and drink suited to its nourishment, so has the soul... Heavenly things cannot support the body; they are not suited to its nature: earthly things cannot support the soul, for the same reason."[62]

One of the popular discussions among some Christians today is about the sin of gluttony. Some Christians are making the claim that we need to spend more time worrying about what our body looks like, and that we can't be Christians unless we cut back on what we take in when we eat. I don't

62   A. Clarke, *Adam Clarke's Commentary Volume 5* (New York: Abingdon-Cokesbury Press, p. 66

know if this is true or not, and I am unconvinced that it is our purpose to spend our time dealing with something so trivial, and something that can be so drastically different for each person. I am convinced that it is not the place of those holding the discussions to judge all other Christians based on the way they look. According the Apostle Paul, exercise is of a little importance because it affects a temporary body, but to develop our spiritual lives is of utmost importance.[63] Throughout the course of history there have been people of all shapes and sizes. Professional football players work out and do whatever is necessary to excel in their position, but of necessity linemen are much different in their physical characteristics than quarterbacks. They are all athletes, but each one exhibits drastically different physical features. If we have a problem with our nourishment in the church today it is not with that of the flesh, but nourishment of our spirits. Our issue is not gluttony, but the polar opposite: starvation!

If we deprive our body of what it needs when we hunger and thirst we are starving ourselves. But what happens when we do the same thing to our spirit? What happens when we long for the joy of the Holy Ghost, or for the peace that surpasses all understanding and do not place ourselves in a position to experience these gifts of God? We have starved ourselves spiritually. And this starvation – just like physical starvation – eventually leads to death. We can never expect to maintain

---

63   1 Timothy 4:8

a relationship with God if we are not willing to nourish the spirit that experiences that relationship, but continually we look around us and see professing Christians starving their souls. They are famished of the things that will provide them the peace that they need to make it through this journey through this hostile, foreign land.

The results of this spiritual starvation are alarming to say the least. People are looking for something deeper, something more, and are not finding it in the church. They are continually turning to other sources. When they do not see professing Christians living with the peace of God in their hearts they turn to the fiction section of their local bookstore. People read thousands of Christian fiction books every year. These books are not inherently bad, in fact, they are much better than a lot of the other things we could use for our entertainment. But these books alone will never sustain our soul. People read book after book and story after story, but many of the same people will never read a book that directs them toward God and His Word. They will never read books that teach us of a deeper spiritual life or encourage us to walk closer with God. They have gorged themselves on junk food and ignored the necessities that will provide their souls the nourishment they need. If it doesn't make them feel good immediately they don't want it. There is a lot of that sentiment floating around the church today and we see the starving spirits to prove it.

Our starvation also causes people to turn away from what is Christian altogether. Whether we want to admit it or not, interest in the occult and its practices among young people is at an all-time high. It is prominent in our entertainment and portrayed as a normal part of life. People are interested in hundreds of godless, pantheistic practices because they don't know where to turn to satisfy the appetite that they have for something spiritual. They understand that there is a need within their heart, but do not know how to fulfill it.

When we ignore the need for spiritual fulfillment our focus turns to the things of the world. We starve our spirits to the point of death, and we no longer acknowledge God or His work. We look to riches and wealth and all the things the world has to offer us, and place ourselves in a land of confusion - a place where we have everything we want and still live without real peace and joy; never having known righteousness. The Bible illustrates such a state by calling it Babylon, a city of great wealth and prosperity, but no god to provide the souls of its inhabitants the peace for which they long. Scripture shows us a great harlot who carries this name, as well as a fallen city that looks to satisfy spiritual appetite with its worldly goods.

"And he carried me away in the Spirit into a wilderness, and I saw a woman sitting on a scarlet beast that was full of blasphemous names…And on her forehead was written a name of mystery: 'Babylon the great, mother of prostitutes and of earth's abominations.'"[64] We read here about one who is given great pleasure by all the temporal things of the world. She is

---

64   Revelation 17:4, 5

dressed in what the world values, and represents what the world seeks, but John's vision went on to describe this further, "After this I saw another angel…And he called out with a mighty voice, 'Fallen, fallen is Babylon the great!'"[65] This shows us what God thinks when we use all the things of the world in an attempt to satisfy our spiritual appetite. Those efforts are fallen! Notice that the Scripture does not say "Babylon has fallen" but that Babylon "is fallen." This is something that was fallen from its beginning! There has never been a day when it was acceptable in the eyes of God to ignore the necessities of our soul. Since the beginning of time our spirits have needed fellowship with God and an experience of His righteousness. Furthermore, it has never been the will of God to starve our souls by ignoring our spiritual hunger and thirst. God has provided what we need, and we must look to Him for fulfillment.

All the things of the world are temporary at best. None of them can ever fulfill the eternal needs of the spirit. "And the merchants of the earth weep and mourn for her [Babylon]… The merchants of these wares, who gained wealth from her, will stand far off…weeping and mourning aloud, 'Alas, alas, for the great city that was clothed in fine linen, in purple and scarlet, adorned with gold, with jewels, and with pearls! For in a single hour all this wealth has been laid waste.'"[66] Our efforts to fulfill our spiritual appetite with worldly things result only in futility and strife. They will bring us to a place of weeping

65 Revelation 18:1, 2
66 Revelation 18:11, 15-17

and mourning, depression and self-pity. Satisfaction will never come from the things of the world, but only from what is spiritual.

Jesus promised that those who hunger and thirst for righteousness will be filled. Our soul does not find fulfillment through worldly goods, but in fellowship with God. "Jesus said, 'I am the bread of life; whoever comes to me shall not hunger, and whoever believes in me shall never thirst.'"[67] No matter where we set our sights, or what we aim to accomplish, God is still our sustainer, and His righteousness is what brings us fulfillment. Dennis Kinlaw speaks to this subject,

> "God is the origin of our life. When we turn away from
> Him, spiritual death begins. It may take a long time,
> but death is inevitable. Do you know what the Holiness
> Movement's message is? It is that God can be the center
> of your life, so that all your life flows from Him."[68]

As we begin to understand our spiritual life we find that our physical existence does not need to steer our spiritual life, but our spiritual life will always have a profound effect on all the rest of our life. Until the longing of our soul is satisfied, nothing else we do will bring contentment. This is why we see such power within the spiritual life. While we must live

---

67   John 6:35

68   Kinlaw, *We Live As Christ*, p. 43

with some of our physical characteristics, God has the power to transform our spiritual life. He can bring about change in every part of our life by developing kingdom characteristics in our spirit through His sanctifying grace.

The righteous character of God is the fulfillment of our hunger and thirst. God promised us, "I will satisfy the weary soul, and every languishing soul I will replenish..."[69] Our satisfaction with life, and the call that has been placed on us as we live in this world, comes as we submit ourselves to God – as we allow Him to dwell in us and establish His values and culture within our hearts. John Wesley wrote, "Righteousness... is the image of God, the mind which was in Christ Jesus. It Is every holy and heavenly temper in one; springing from, as well as terminating in the love of God, as our Father and Redeemer, and the love of all men for his sake."[70] We can search the world for all it has to offer us, but unless we experience the righteousness of God in our hearts we will never know fulfillment, peace, or joy. The fulfillment of God's people as they walk with Him in righteousness is the one beacon of hope that exists for this lost and dying world. God desires to place His character in our hearts and our fulfillment comes from the overflow of that character which pours from our spirit into the lives of those around us. It comes from carrying the culture of heaven to earth.

---

69   Jeremiah 31:25

70   Wesley, *The Works of John Wesley Volume 5*, p. 267

The righteous are blessed, not always with worldly goods, but with the satisfaction that comes from knowing they have a purpose and are here for a reason, and seeing that purpose fulfilled as God's righteousness shines forth from them. Martyn Lloyd-Jones reminded us, "They alone are truly happy who are seeking to be righteous. Put happiness in the place of righteousness and you will never get it."[71]

Today's Christians are offered the peace that comes with knowing that whether we have little or much, God is working through us. Our creator has chosen you and I to be the vessels of His culture and kingdom. That's why the Psalmist wrote, "Better is the little that the righteous has than the abundance of the wicked. For the arms of the wicked shall be broken, but the Lord upholds the righteous."[72] That is also why Jesus taught us to, "Seek first the kingdom of God and his righteousness..."[73] We spend far too much time worrying about temporary things even though Jesus promised that if we spend our days seeking the righteousness of God all those things would be provided. In fact, He told the people that the Gentiles (or pagans) seek after the things of the world, but God has called us to a better life than that. A holy life.

The Old Testament continually reminds us that if we seek God with all our hearts we will find Him. It is out of a great hunger and thirst for His character and will that we seek Him.

---

71   Lloyd-Jones, *Studies In the Sermon On the Mount*, p. 75
72   Psalm 37:16, 17
73   Matthew 6:33

This hunger and thirst of our spirit is a result of being spiritually alive. "Unless a man is born again he cannot see the kingdom…"[74] If I'm not mistaken, you are alive once you are born. If we cannot find within us any desire to know more of God, to be with His people, or to experience His righteousness it is for one reason: we are dead! Leonard Ravenhill once said, "We have as much of God as we want today."[75] We no longer see His righteousness because we have lost our appetite for it. Just as the overwhelming heat of a scorching summer day diminishes our physical appetite, we have allowed the things of the world to starve our spirit to a point near death. How long will we allow this to go on? When will we awaken to our need?

God instructed the prophet Isaiah, "Tell the righteous that it shall be well with them, for they shall eat the fruit of their deeds."[76] We read about the satisfaction of the righteous and the blessed life that they will live, but are we willing to do what is necessary to fulfill our spiritual appetite? When so many thousands of Christians struggle through life to find fulfillment, can we honestly say that we have the spiritual appetite for righteousness that comes with being born of the spirit?

---

74 John 3:3

75 I found this quote early in my ministry and it has stuck with me. I cannot locate the specific text where it was originally found, but whether or not it was Ravenhill who made the statement does not change its truth.

76 Isaiah 3:10

The Apostle Paul wanted to be in the holy presence of God so badly that it drove him to tell the Philippian church, "For me to live is Christ, and to die is gain."[77] We all want to die like the righteous, with hope and anticipation of life to come, but for this to happen we must live like the righteous. We must fulfill more than our bodily appetite; Christians must search for spiritual fulfillment in Jesus Christ. Can you honestly say today that you are satisfied? This is a blessing that Christ promised, but is it a blessing that has become part of the culture of your life?

---

77 Philippians 1:21

Blessed Are the Merciful

Blessed are the merciful, for they shall receive mercy.
-Matthew 5:7

The story has been told of a politician who became enraged when he looked at proofs of photos he recently had taken by a local photographer. He called the photographer and complained, "These pictures do not do me justice!" The photographer replied, "Justice?!?! With a face like that you need mercy!"[78]

It is a humbling to acknowledge this fact, but every person on the face of the earth stands in need of mercy at some point in their life. I always find it interesting when I hear someone say that they quit attending church because they have been "hurt by the people." They get angry about some action or comment that may or may not have been justified and spend the rest of their lives nursing a grudge against the people of God. That attitude gives the impression that they believe those who hurt

---

78   I have heard this story told in many settings and with many variations over the years. Therefore, I will not credit anyone specific, but do not take credit myself.

them are the only people who have ever hurt anyone. And they are implying to us that they believe they have never done anything that causes them to stand in need of mercy, but that is simply not true.

If we look at the order of the beatitudes we see that this issue of mercy is where our visible separation from the world begins. To this point we have looked at the need to possess a Christian heart in this definition of God's culture: poverty of spirit, a realization of the gravity of sin that drives us to mourn, a meek and willing heart, and a desire for righteousness above the things of the world. All of those things happen within our soul and are a result of walking closer with God each day. But if we are really going to claim to hold a different set of values than the world around us there must be evidence of these values in our lives. The things we work for, the way we spend our time and energy, and the way we view the world must be different from those who have not experienced the culture of God's kingdom. So where do we start?

The world we live in teaches us to look out for ourselves above all else. We put ourselves first and do whatever is necessary to find what we perceive to be happiness, and if someone does something that hinders our pleasure or gets in our way we make them pay for it. We live in a world that is bent on vengeance. Communities, cultures and nations have been changed over the course of history because of our desire to get even with those we believe have wronged us somehow. The world values this attitude, and the greater the damage we can inflict in return for the trespasses of others, the more esteemed we become in the eyes of our society. The idea that someone might act like Christ and "turn the other cheek"[79] is completely foreign to such a culture.

The culture of God's kingdom stands against the world's need for revenge. Jesus teaches us in the beatitudes that we are not to begrudgingly show mercy (as so many often do if they show mercy at all), but that we will be blessed for being merciful. Those who show mercy to others will be truly happy and fulfilled, and God's blessing will rest on them, but not those who show a half-hearted mercy that continues to bring up the wrongs of the past. God's blessing is for those who will show the same mercy that God has shown to us.

To be merciful is to understand that mercy originated with God Himself. Before we show mercy to others we must first understand that we have stood before God in need of His mercy. Before our lives were turned over to Him we were sinners. We had transgressed His law and turned our backs on His love. We had done nothing to earn His favor or His forgiveness for our sin, but He gave it to us anyway. God became our example of mercy and forgiveness, that's why the Apostle John could write, "Grace, mercy, and peace will be with us, from God the Father and from Jesus Christ the Father's Son, in truth and love."[80] We look not within ourselves when we feel like someone has

79 Matthew 5:39

80 2 John 1:3

done something wrong to us, but to God. We look for His direction and the guidance of His Spirit. The mercy that we show others comes from the source of all mercy: Almighty God! "But the wisdom that comes down from above is first pure, then peaceable, gentle, open to reason, full of mercy and good fruits, impartial and sincere."[81] When the God who authored mercy instills His character and the culture of His Kingdom in us we will see something happen in our lives that seems impossible in the societies of this world: we will become merciful.

The entirety of Scripture reminds us of God's mercy. The Old Testament sacrificial system seemed gruesome and terrifying, but it was an object lesson in the mercy of God. The one who made the sacrifice placed their hand on the head of the animal as it was killed by the priests. They had to physically touch it while the blood that gave it life was drained from its body and its vitality slowly slipped away. Through that sacrifice man was shown the gravity of sin. "The wages of sin is death."[82] It showed the results of our fractured fellowship with God as the essence of the life of that animal disappeared and its body began to weaken and eventually fade into death. This sacrifice resulted from that person's sin, and they were a part of the death that they experienced through that act. But the one who deserved that death was not the animal, it was the person!

This ritual did more than simply illustrate the gravity of sin

81   James 3:17

82   Romans 6:23

(though it did illustrate it); it also showed the depths of God's mercy toward us. We talk a lot about what people deserve, but what does anyone really deserve? On my very best day I still cannot make up for the sins that were committed in my life. Only the blood of Jesus Christ does that. What I deserve is far less than the mercy God has shown me in saving my soul. You will find that each of us stands in that position before God. If we are going to show mercy to others, we need to remind ourselves that we "deserve" no more or less than they do. It is only by God's mercy that we stand in His service today proclaiming His culture to the world.

Most of the time the mercy we show has boundaries and limitations placed on it; boundaries that we have created. That has never been the intention of God; the mercy Jesus instructed us to show is the same boundless mercy and love that God has shown to us. It is more than mercy to our families and our friends, but a mercy that extends to all those with whom we might come into contact. "But I say to you, love your enemies and pray for those who persecute you. For if you love those who love you, what reward do you have? Do not even the tax collectors do the same?"[83] Even when asked specifically how many times one must be forgiven Jesus proclaimed an uninhibited mercy. "Then Peter came up and said to him, 'Lord, how often will my brother sin against me, and I forgive

---

83   Matthew 5:44, 46

him? As many as seven times?' Jesus said to him, 'I do not say to you seven times, but seventy times seven.'"[84]

Mercy and forgiveness go together in our Christian lives. We are called to display both as part of the culture that God instills within us as His people. As we make our way through this world, this Christ-like mercy must be a normal response to the circumstances we confront. Mercy is shown when we experience inadequate service at a restaurant and leave a tip anyway, or we are willing to overlook it when we return home from the grocery store and realize that the cashier short-changed us 39 cents.[85] Many of the things that happen to us are not deliberate attempts by others to cause us harm. It is most often simply oversight on their part, and sometimes oversensitivity on our part. We have become a very thin-skinned nation, and it shows when we so easily take offense to things that happen to us. The people around us may do something that we do not like, or even something that hurts us, but many of them mean well.

We must remember that we don't always know what circumstances are surrounding the lives of those with whom we come into contact. Some may be going through a great difficulty – greater than we will ever understand – and the mercy that is shown to them by God's people is what they

---

84   Matthew 18:21, 22

85   I am aware that these examples seem like they are over the top, but I have had conversations with professing Christians who took great offense to these very circumstances.

needed to get them through the day. Even in the cases of the ones who have sinned and hurt us purposely it is not you and I against whom they sinned. First and foremost, they have sinned against God. David knew this when he said, "Against you, you only, have I sinned and done what is evil in your sight, so that you may be justified in your words and blameless in your judgment."[86] David proclaimed that it is God's judgment that is just, not ours. It is our responsibility to create a culture of mercy and forgiveness, not punishment.

When we deal with this issue, it is important for us to realize what it means to show mercy to the larger body of the church as well as to individuals. Sometimes we must have compassion on the entire church and relieve her of burdensome issues by dealing with a difficulty caused by a single individual, or a small group of individuals. When difficulties arise we must forgive those who have caused them, but we cannot allow them to continue to cause division or strife in the church. When things that hinder the well-being of the church become patterns of behavior rather than isolated occurrences then mercy must be shown to the church by relieving the problem. We would do well to remember that Jonah was thrown off the ship so that God could save the ship and Jonah! If he had not been thrown overboard, God's work would not have taken place in his heart and life. There are times that God uses such a circumstance to teach the church as well as those who must be disciplined. We

86   Psalm 51:4

do not do this lightly, but soberly and with devout conviction that it is indeed the will of God. The motive behind even this type of action is to show God's mercy.

As daunting as this task sounds, mercy must become a normal operation in the Christian life. It cannot be something we turn on and off, but something that is a part of who we are. Martyn Lloyd-Jones taught us, "Anything controlled by us, whether lifeless or lively, is not Christianity. Christianity is that which controls us, which masters us, which happens to us."[87] When we are saved, and born of the kingdom, our values must change. We do not choose which passages of Scripture we want to believe, but we surrender ourselves to whatever God reveals to us through His Word. Too many Christians today live by the principles and values of the culture of God's kingdom when it's convenient, but when it benefits them to live as the world these kingdom values no longer show. We seem to take up and put down our Christianity at will, and we see a powerless church as a result; a church that has lost the ability to effect any real change in the society around us.

The beatitudes taught by Jesus are a part of who we are. They follow us everywhere we go because they have been established in our hearts and lives by the Spirit of God. This is why our values become so drastically different from those of the world. When we submit ourselves to God's reign over our

---

87 M. Lloyd-Jones, *Authentic Christianity* (Wheaton: Crossway Books, 2000), p. 22

hearts we are no longer stumbling through this dark world looking for hope, but we are living in the overflow of God's Spirit – our guide – as we walk the path before us. God's Spirit invades the world through the lives that we live; His character and work are unmistakable in the lives of those who surrender to Him. Our humble spirit and mournful heart, our meekness and desire for righteousness bring us to the place where mercy can be shown to those who do not know God but desperately need Him – through us!

These characteristics of mercy and forgiveness help us to live as Christian witnesses in the world around us, and they help us to live with one another as God's church. "Put on then, as God's chosen ones, holy and beloved, compassionate hearts, kindness, humility, meekness, and patience, bearing with one another, and if one has a complaint against another, forgiving each other; as the Lord has forgiven you, so you also must forgive."[88]

When we show such mercy we experience nothing less than the reward of God: His mercy. Our willingness to display mercy helps us to see those around us as God sees them. We see the church as His children. We see the world as those who are lost and in need of the mercy that we have received. This merciful attitude toward others places us in God's favor as we learn the command of Jesus, "Go and learn what this means,

---

88 Colossians 3:12, 13

'I desire mercy, and not sacrifice.'"[89] We will find that, as the values of God's kingdom become a part of our lives, mercy will provide us with a happiness and fulfillment that vengeance can never supply. We can spend a lifetime seeking revenge on others, but it is mercy that will provide us the experience of heaven here on earth.

Scripture tells us that we love because He first loved us.[90] God showed His mercy to us while we were dead in sin. We had committed treason against our King and spurned His love, but God forgave us nonetheless, because He is merciful. People of the world see God at work in us, and through our lives. God began a relationship with us by showing us mercy. If our first experience with God was His mercy and that is the one thing we most often refuse to show others, how will they ever see Him? Furthermore, how many blessings might we be missing as a result of our failure to show mercy? Just imagine the countless possibilities of God's blessing on the merciful.

---

89   Matthew 9:13

90   1 John 4:19

Blessed Are the Pure In Heart

Blessed are the pure in heart, for they shall see God.
-Matthew 5:8

Why do people go to the store and buy bottles of water when it is so readily available? All of us have access to water that is better than what is available to most of the people in the world, yet many of us buy our drinking water in bottles. What would drive us to do such a thing? Purity! When I buy a bottle of water, I expect (though there is question as to the validity of this assumption) that the only thing in that container is pure water. There are no impurities like we might find in water that comes from a well. There is nothing there except for the elements of hydrogen and oxygen that make up water. If I get a glass from the tap there is no guarantee that water is the only thing in the glass, but when it comes from a company that bottles pure water I should be able to expect one single thing in the bottle that I have purchased.

This principle illustrates for us the character that God wants to establish in our hearts. When we discuss purity we are talking about a oneness in our hearts, and in our purposes and motives. It is this focus of motive that John Wesley described as "Christian perfection." The command of Jesus later in the fifth chapter of Matthew is, "You therefore must be perfect, as your heavenly father is perfect."[91] This does not mean that we are flawless, but that our heart is oriented toward one thing: the values of God's kingdom. It shows our preparation to fulfill our purpose. When we look at the context of the command, Jesus was not commanding His people to be perfect in all things, but in love. The love that God has shown us should emanate from our hearts and permeate the culture that we live in our everyday lives. That is our purpose, and the one thing on which our hearts should be focused.

Look at it this way: I collect guns. I have one particular rifle that I got from a family member. This gun looks awful. It has some rust on it and looks like it has been well used over the years, and it bothers me to own a gun that looks that bad. I wish there was a way to fix it and make it look like new again, but it is not possible. To do such a thing would decrease its value. However, despite the terrible appearance of that gun it still perfectly accomplishes the purpose for which

91   Matthew 5:48

it was created. When sighted properly and shot by someone who knows how to aim and fire correctly, it will hit the target at which it is aimed every time. Therefore, when we look at it based on purpose, it is perfect.

Mildred Bangs Wynkoop tells us, "The 'faith' on which purity depends contradicts anything that human merit might achieve and points to the obedience of total capitulation to and dependence upon God – a single heart."[92] There is a reason I don't use that gun – or any other gun – to hit a golf ball. It was not created for that purpose! When the purity of our motives is compromised, we are no longer focused on the purpose to which God has called us – to live His heavenly culture. Purity is not stained with peripheral desires, but is focused entirely on God and His kingdom. This is why Scripture says, "for the one who doubts is like a wave of the sea that is driven and tossed by the wind. For that person must not suppose that he will receive anything from the Lord; he is a double-minded man, unstable in all his ways."[93] James goes on to instruct us, "Draw near to God, and he will draw near to you. Cleanse your hands, you sinners, and purify your hearts, you double-minded."[94] Scripture places great value on oneness of mind. God has taught us the importance of focusing on our purpose and maintaining the purity of that cause.

92   M Wynkoop, *A Theology of Love*, (Kansas City: Beacon Hill Press, 1972), p. 262

93   James 1:6-8

94   James 4:8

Purity means that even interest in one's self has subsided in favor of God's will. Too often God's purposes are only important as long as they do not affect our will and desire. This self-will is nothing more than a distraction from God's culture. It affects our relationships and our ability to serve God's kingdom fully. We spend a great deal of time worrying about our own happiness, we even tell ourselves, "I deserve to be happy." The truth of the matter is, none of us really want what we actually deserve. It is a blessing to each of us to put off our selfishness and bring all of our desires into a oneness around God's purpose. This comes from seeing, through our relationship with Jesus Christ, the desires that God has for us. It comes from experiencing His provision and work as we walk with Him and bring our will under subjection to His reign over His kingdom. Dennis Kinlaw wrote, "Until a person knows fellowship with the living Lord, he cannot be delivered from the self-interest that tyrannizes him, contaminating his life and relationships."[95]

Purity is the focus that we have on the culture of God, and the place in which this culture operates is our heart. The heart represents the entirety of our being, and all that we are. Martyn Lloyd-Jones commented, "According to the general scriptural usage of the term, the heart means the center of the

---

95 Kinlaw, *We Live As Christ*, p. 19

personality. It does not merely mean the seat of the affections and emotions."[96]

Too many Christians in our day look pure outwardly while living anything but a pure, holy life. We must be pure in heart if we are going to live in fellowship with a Holy God. There are many people whose actions are not inherently bad, but if those actions come from impure hearts they will never please God. Some take part in charity work to make themselves feel good, and many do good things for others with the expectation of something in return. Scripture teaches us that the only works pleasing to God are those which come from the purity of our hearts. "Having purified your souls by your obedience to the truth for a sincere brotherly love, love one another earnestly from a pure heart…"[97] Jesus said, "You blind Pharisee! First clean the inside of the cup and the plate, that the outside also may be clean."[98] C.W. Naylor said this about the issue of heart purity: "A pure and holy inner life issues in a pure and blameless outer life, devoted to service and helpfulness. This is the religion that is a well-watered land, full of fruitfulness. It is a land of song and cheer and of true blessedness."[99]

Why is our heart so important? It bears such significance because this is origin of all our motives. "Keep your heart

---

96   Lloyd-Jones, *Studies In the Sermon on the Mount*, p. 109

97   1 Peter 1:22

98   Matthew 23:26

99   C. Naylor, *The Secret of the Singing Heart*, (Anderson: Warner Press), p. 16

with all diligence, for out of it spring the issues of life."[100] Our values, culture and world-view are all matters of our heart. The culture that we live is a direct indicator of the heart we possess. Consider our purpose as Paul conveyed it to Timothy, "The aim of our charge is love that issues from a pure heart and a good conscience and a sincere faith."[101] If the culture that we are currently living in our homes, and that which goes with us to the work place or school is not God's culture, the problem is in our heart! We have not allowed the purity of God – His oneness of purpose – to be firmly established there by His Spirit. The actions of our lives are a result of what comes from within. Consider the words of A.W. Tozer, "The fountain of spirituality flows outward. You cannot contaminate a fountain, because the fountain within shall flow out. Any contagion or infection that comes from the outside is automatically rendered new by the outflow. If it came from the world, it could bring its pollution with it; but because it is the outflow from within him, it is not affected by the world."[102] This is how we can claim a purity of heart, because, "I have been crucified with Christ. It is no longer I who live, but Christ who lives in me..."[103] We are pure of heart, when our motives come from the Spirit of God who lives in our hearts.

---

100 Proverbs 4:23

101 1 Timothy 1:5

102 Tozer, *Reclaiming Christianity*, p. 83

103 Galatians 2:20

The remarkable thing about purity of heart is not simply that it is possible - its remarkability lies in its reward. Jesus told us that those who are pure in heart shall "see God." The Greek from which this is translated literally means that we are to *gaze on something remarkable.* It does not derive from the same word that was used to voluntarily look on something, but it is something that cannot help but be noticed. This is why Jesus said confidently that when our hearts are pure we will see God. He did not say that we might, or that we could, but that we will. When our motives are to promote and live His culture we will begin to see Him work in places that we had never seen before. We will experience His work in ways that we have never imagined. Even as he was martyred, Stephen saw the work of God. "But he, full of the Holy Spirit, gazed into heaven and saw the glory of God, and Jesus standing at the right hand of God. And he said, 'Behold, I see the heavens opened, and the Son of Man standing at the right hand of God.'"[104]

Christians today, just as the Jews of Old Testament times, expect to see God. They want to see His work, but have so often forgotten that His work issues from a pure heart. The Jews tried to conjure God's work through their tradition and ritual. The Christians of our day continually lower the standard of what God's work should be to meet their limited experience. Rather than purifying their hearts, they claim the work of God in

---

104 Acts 7:55, 56

things that are not worthy of God, and many times in things that can just as easily be accomplished without God.

Those with a pure heart are the people who should rightly expect to see God. When the purpose of man becomes the service of his rightful King, the work of God is seen through that life by the world around us. "O Lord, who shall sojourn in your tent? Who shall dwell on your holy hill? He who walks blamelessly and does what is right and speaks truth in his heart…"[105] It is through this purity of motive that the world around us understands the need for God's work in their lives. Interaction with those of pure hearts brings Jesus Christ and His culture into this world. Dennis Kinlaw tells us, "If it is true that, wherever I am, Christ himself is present, then He must do something in my life far more than simply take away the penalty of my sins. He must make me in some way an image of himself. He must transform me into a kind of channel through which He can come into my world."[106]

Many contemporary theologians and preachers have diminished the possibility of heart purity in this life, and by doing so have diminished the command – and as a result, the blessing – of God. They claim that sin is just too powerful to be completely overcome. They tell us that with each passing day the sin of the world drives our motives and controls our actions. Nothing could be further from the truth. These same

105 Psalm 15:1, 2
106 Kinlaw, *We Live As Christ*, p. 48

people wonder why we see so little of the power of God at work in the world today. The answer is simple: our hearts are not pure! Our motives do not come from a love for God and His kingdom, but from a love for ourselves and our sin. Michael Lodahl wrote, "Many holiness theologians in recent centuries have claimed that it is possible to overcome sin in this life. Our suggestion that we can be perfect in any particular moment when we respond in love to God's call of love offers a realistic way to affirm this claim. After all, when we love as God calls, we do not sin. Because of God's enabling in each moment in our lives, sin is not inevitable. Love is always possible."[107]

Oneness in motive and desire is the requirement if we are to experience God's work. We look around at the numerous things that we believe keep us from experiencing God's power, but we need look no further than within. "Blessed are the pure in heart, for they shall see God."

---

107 T. Oord and M. Lodahl, *Relational Holiness*, (Kansas City: Beacon Hill Press, 2005), p. 135

Blessed Are the Peacemakers

Blessed are the peacemakers, for they shall be called sons of God.
-Matthew 5:9

The previous beatitude said, "Blessed are the pure in heart..." We have discovered that this purity is a oneness of heart and a focus of our motives. The desire that drives us is to please God and live as part of His kingdom. This oneness brings us a peace as we live by faith in the provision of our King. We realize that we cannot control the circumstances around us, but we can control our dependence upon God and, therefore, the peace within our hearts as we encounter the various circumstances of life. When we look around and see war ravaged nations, economies on the brink of collapse, and social issues that grieve the heart of God we still live with a peace that comes from understanding that God is still our King, and we are citizens of a kingdom that transcends even the most overwhelming circumstances this life might present.

The peacemaker does more than live with this peace, he

models it to those around him. If we are to be a peacemaker, we must first possess the peace of God in our own hearts. We must live as those who have overcome the fear and worry of the world realizing that "God gave us a spirit not of fear but of power and love and self-control."[108]

The peace in our heart must show clearly in the way we live; to the extent that it begins to affect the lives of others as it brings them into a relationship with the author of all peace. Adam Clarke wrote,

> "A peacemaker is a man who, being endowed with a generous public spirit, labors for the public good, and feels his own interest promoted in promoting that of others: therefore, instead of fanning the fire of strife, he uses his influence and wisdom to reconcile the contending parties, adjust their differences, and restore them to a state of unity. As all men are represented to be in a state of hostility to God and each other, the Gospel is called the Gospel of peace, because it tends to reconcile men to God and to each other."[109]

A peacemaker is more than one who mediates a settlement between men and women who oppose one another, but one who first and foremost helps restore their relationships with God.

---

108 2 Timothy 1:7

109 Clarke, *Adam Clarke's Commentary Volume 5*, p. 67

As we look at the world around us we see a myriad of reasons to live without peace. The words of Jesus in Matthew 24:6 are continually fulfilled, "And you will hear of wars and rumors of wars. See that you are not alarmed, for this must take place, but the end is not yet." The events that take place around us constantly distract and divide the race of man. They divide us from one another and distract us from the work of God that is taking place in the world through the people of His kingdom. We miss God's work when we allow ourselves to get bogged down in the trials and tribulation of the world while forgetting that God has more for us than to be shackled by difficulty and strife. Jesus told us, "In the world you will have tribulation. But take heart; I have overcome the world."[110] Through every struggle, and over every obstacle marches the kingdom of God. These things need not deter us as we live in the peace of God because all of them have been overcome in the person and work of Jesus Christ. The power of God, working through us, cannot be stopped by the ways of man, the rulers of the earth, or even spiritual principalities who would discourage us as we live under the rule and reign of Jesus Christ our Lord.

As the world continues to divide and distract, the peace of God brings a culture of unity and restoration to the people of the kingdom. God does not promise us temporal prosperity, but spiritual peace, that's why the Apostle Paul wrote, "the kingdom of God is not a matter of eating and drinking but of

---

110 John 16:33

righteousness and peace and joy in the Holy Spirit."[111] Entrance into God's kingdom gives us rest from the worries of the world around us and from the weariness that comes with the fear in which so many Americans live today. In spite of the anxiety caused by the media and politicians of our day, a peacemaker lives within the peaceful values of the kingdom and displays those values to all those who interact with them. They are not driven by the terror of the world around them, but by a desire to invade this world with a culture that originated in the heights of heaven rather than those derived from the depths of the heart of sinful man.

The sin that dwells in the heart of man is what must be overcome if we are to make peace between man and God. D.A. Carson commented on this,

> "Within the total biblical framework, the greatest peacemaker is Jesus Christ – the Prince of Peace. He makes peace between God and man by removing sin, the ground of alienation; he makes peace between man and man both by removing sin and by bringing men into a right relationship with God."[112]

A peacemaker is not one who simply appeases the world, but one who stands firmly against the sin that is valued by the world. They do not ignore broken relationships between God

---

111 Romans 14:17

112 D. Carson, *Jesus' Sermon on the Mount* (Grand Rapids: Baker Books, 1987), p. 27

and man, but work to restore that relationship to a fellowship between man and his creator.

What are we doing today to model a right relationship with God to others? Are we trusting in Him like Scripture commands? Do we live by faith, and have we overcome the fear that drives so many? If we are to inherit the promise that comes with peacemaking we must answer these questions affirmatively.

Those who make and promote peace in the lives of others are classified as "children of God." They are promoting what comes from the God who has authored all peace. Those who show this characteristic of God are indeed worthy to be called His children. As we live in the peace, Scripture tells us, "The Holy Spirit bears witness with our spirit that we are children of God…"[113]

On the other hand, those who perpetrate division, strife, and fear are also children of their father. "You are of your father the devil, and your will is to do your father's desires."[114] There are people all over America today who profess to be Christians while allowing their lives and their witness to be driven by utter fear of the world around them.

When I was growing up my friends and I used to spend countless hours in the woods on summer afternoons swinging from grapevines that grew in the trees. We had a great time,

113 Romans 8:16
114 John 8:44

but today that's considered too dangerous. Many parents live in fear that someone may get hurt. We allow our fear to drive the decisions we make and the things we do. Countless marriages fall apart because parents allow their fear to keep them from letting their children – who are grown and married – live their own lives. Their fear causes them to interfere in marriages and in the lives of grandchildren when they should not.

Some go even further. They like to see others stirred up and will stop at nothing to cause drama and discord among God's people. They play individuals against one another and ultimately have a terrible effect on the spiritual lives of those around them, all the while claiming to be citizens of God's kingdom. The culture that surrounds them is anything but the peaceful culture of the kingdom.

Make no mistake, the world is offended by those who hold to the values of God's kingdom. They will call us naïve, and sometimes even negligent, when we live with God's peace in our hearts. But the reward is greater than any cost; how can we spurn the idea of being children of God? "See what kind of love the Father has given to us, that we should be called children of God; and so we are. The reason why the world does not know us is that it did not know him."[115]

How can man be worthy of such a reward? How can we bear such a title as God's children? It is because the very character of

115 1 John 3:1

God is displayed through our lives for the entire world to see. Those who live with peace in their hearts are the very people with whom God wants to be identified. They do not simply live peaceable lives themselves, but they bring others into harmony with God's peace through their witness and example. In spite of criticism from the world around them they continue to create a culture that runs counter to the values, beliefs, and standards of the world.

Through the conduct and actions of peacemakers God's work is evident. Through their speech, their priorities, and even their relationships, people see values that have come from heaven to earth. Many experience the invasion of God's kingdom through their interaction with a single life of peace. The influence of such a peaceful life is beyond human explanation. That is why James told us, "The harvest of righteousness is sown in peace by those who make peace."[116] God has called each of us to a righteous life in His kingdom, and the result of this righteousness is a peace that surpasses our knowledge and understanding.

If we are to be peacemakers we must first experience the peace that comes with God's righteousness as it emanates from our hearts. We talk about the peace of God, sing about it, and pray for it, but do we live it? When others look at our lives, do they see God's peace? Do they see His kingdom?

For the first two years of my ministry I had the opportunity

---

116 James 3:18

to lead God's people as they worship, and it is always a joy to listen to them sing the great truths of our Lord. Though I enjoy the contemporary music of my generation, my favorite song remains one that was written years ago by Barney Warren and it speaks of the peace of God's kingdom culture in our lives. Consider the words that describe this kingdom:

> There's a theme that is sweet to my mem'ry,
> There's a joy that I cannot express,
> There's a treasure that gladdens my being,
> 'Tis the kingdom of God's righteousness.

> There's a scene of its grandness before me,
> Of its greatness there can be no end;
> It is joy, it is peace, it is glory,
> In my heart, how these riches do blend!

> I am lost in its splendor and beauty,
> To its ne'er-fading heights I would rise,
> Till I see the King come to receive me,
> And explore it with Him in the skies.

> What a pleasure in life it is bringing!
> What assurance and hope ever bright!
> O what rapture and bliss are awaiting,
> When our faith shall be lost in the sight!

'Tis a kingdom of peace, it is reigning within,
It shall ever increase in my soul;
We possess it right here when He saves from all sin,
And 'twill last while the ages shall roll.

-Barney Warren, *The Kingdom of Peace*[117]

---

117 A. Newell and R. Vader (ed.), *Worship the Lord Hymnal* (Anderson: Warner Press, 1989), p. 481

Blessed Are the Persecuted

Blessed are those who are persecuted for righteousness'
sake, for theirs is the kingdom of heaven. Blessed are you
when others revile you and persecute you and utter all
kinds of evil against you falsely on my account. Rejoice
and be glad, for your reward is great in heaven, for so
they persecuted the prophets who were before you.
-Matthew 5:10-12

On July 11, 2012, Michael Salman found himself in prison in Phoenix, Arizona. He had not committed any of the heinous crimes that we so often see in America today. He was not a murderer or a thief; he had not embezzled money, and was not even guilty of jaywalking. Salman was imprisoned for breaking a number of Phoenix zoning laws when he hosted a Bible study in his own home. For his crime he was sentenced to 60 days in prison, three years of probation, and was fined $12,180.[118]

118 Accessed July 18, 2012 at: http://foxnewsinsider.com/tag/michael-salman/

The culture we live as Christians has come under scrutiny in recent years. The values God instills in our hearts are called into question, and the motives that lead to our actions and lifestyles are looked on with concern and skepticism. The world does not understand the culture of God's kingdom, and what they do understand offends them. The unselfish lives lived by God's people draw a stark contrast with the selfishness of the society around them, causing society to ridicule and scorn the lives that God has called us to live. This brings about exactly what Scripture predicted – persecution!

Christians today do everything in their power to avoid persecution of any kind. They compromise their convictions at times, and condone many of the sinful things that have become so much a part of the culture of the world. They bow to the norms of society and tiptoe through life trying to hide the work that God is trying to do in and through them. But what good are these convictions if we are so willing to compromise them? Does it really benefit the kingdom of God if we claim to be citizens while continuing to live like the culture that surrounds us? We have forgotten the teaching of Scripture that tells us we must live in the world, but we are not supposed to be of the world. "They are not of the world, just as I am not of the world."[119] What good has all this compromise with worldly culture done anyway? It may be a blow to our ego to consider this fact, but no matter who we are or how much we

---

119 John 17:16

compromise the Word of God, there is someone somewhere who hates us. There are people on this earth who want to destroy us and the culture that God has given us to promote. From the time God established His own people this has been the case.

The Old Testament prophets faced persecution as they carried the messages of God to those who did not want to listen. They were beaten and even killed because God's Word was so offensive to the world. Jeremiah told us about this, "Therefore thus says the Lord concerning the men of Anathoth, who seek your life, and say, 'Do not prophesy in the name of the Lord, or you will die by our hand...'"[120] Jesus even looked back on these people and lamented their animosity toward those who delivered the Word of God to Israel. "Therefore I send you prophets and wise men and scribes, some of whom you will kill and crucify, and some you will flog in your synagogues and persecute from town to town."[121]

The persecution of God's people was not limited to the Old Testament. Jesus told us very plainly that we would face persecution. "I have said these things to you, that in me you may have peace. In the world you will have tribulation. But take heart; I have overcome the world."[122] Do we realize what this means? We spend countless hours trying to make the gospel palatable to the world so that we might avoid persecution, and

---

120 Jeremiah 11:21

121 Matthew 23:24

122 John 16:33

we do it in direct contrast to the teaching of Jesus Christ. How arrogant have we become to believe that Jesus was persecuted and even crucified, but we can find a way to handle this sinful world in a better – and safer- way than He did? Jesus carried this idea a step further in Luke 6:26, "Woe to you, when all people speak well of you, for so their fathers did to the false prophets." Did you notice what He said? Jesus said, "Woe to you," when all men speak well of you. If we are not facing some type of opposition, or persecution, we are not really living the culture that God has sent from heaven to invade this world.

The church has always dealt with persecution, even from the earliest days. "And there arose on that day a great persecution against the church in Jerusalem, and they were all scattered throughout the regions of Judea and Samaria, except the apostles."[123] These men and women left their homes and all that they knew to live the culture of God's kingdom here on earth. "Now those who were scattered because of the persecution that arose over Stephen traveled as far as Phoenicia and Cyprus and Antioch…"[124] Even when they went to various cities to preach they were met with persecution. "But the Jews incited the devout women of high standing and the leading men of the city, stirred up persecution against Paul and Barnabas, and drove them out of their district."[125]

If we are going to live God's culture of heaven on earth, we

---

123 Acts 8:1

124 Acts 11:19

125 Acts 13:50

must come to terms with the idea that we will face persecution. It is not something we can escape, and Scripture makes no provision for compromise to avoid it.

We face persecution because it is a blessing to us. "But even if you should suffer for righteousness sake, you will be blessed. Have no fear of them, nor be troubled…"[126] It is easy to serve God in the absence of hardship. When things go smoothly and all our plans come together we are content to claim that we serve God, but many times when a difficulty arises during these good times we run from it. Our first reaction is to avoid the trouble and try very hard to get away from it, but in doing this we are robbing God of the opportunity to bless us. Persecution and trials are a chance for God to strengthen our faith in Him by delivering us through something that we could never handle on our own. How many times do we deny ourselves the blessing of a growing, active faith by compromising the convictions God has given us so that we can elude trial?

If we go to such lengths to avoid the testing of our faith, and the persecution of the world, how do we know that we are on the right path? If Jesus told us that our lifestyle will offend the world, but we avoid this offense, are we really living a culture that stands in opposition to that of the world? Can it really be said that our values are different than those of the world? The Apostle Paul told us, "Do not be conformed to this world, but

___
126 1 Peter 3:14

be transformed…"[127] This is what offends those around us. This transformation in our lives brings about conviction of their own self-centered, self-serving lives.

When we begin to live according to God's values we are accused of hypocrisy and harboring a judgmental attitude. Every time we point out the standard of the Word of God people remind us of the lives we used to live. Others tell us that we have no right to judge them. At times it seems that the only Scripture the culture of the world knows is Matthew 7:1, "Judge not, that you be not judged." This is taken completely out of context. If we read further, Jesus said in verse 2, "For with the judgment you pronounce you will be judged…"

What is the standard for Christians? It is the Word of God! If we are proclaiming the Word of God we are not judging anyone, God already did that and revealed His judgment to us! Don't ever tell someone they are guilty of judging you because they have cited God's Word. Even Christians accuse others of such things, but if the standard is Scripture the bar will not be lowered because we refuse to point it out to others in fear of judging them.

The world uses arguments such as judgment and hypocrisy, and today even bigotry in an effort to beat down the culture of God. On August 1, 2012, Chick-fil-a restaurants had the greatest day the company has ever experienced. Thousands of people flocked to these establishments in support of the

---

127 Romans 1:22

CEO and his statement supporting the biblical definition of marriage. The statement set off a media firestorm and put the company under great duress from elected government officials in various cities. Many protest the position of this company because it is contrary to the worldliness that has overwhelmed our society, but those who support a different culture came out en mass to support this stand for a different kind of culture and a change in values from the status quo.

Persecution strengthens our faith, and it also earns us reward from God in heaven. Consider the words of Jesus, "Blessed are you when people hate you and when they exclude you and revile you and spurn your name as evil, on account of the Son of Man! Rejoice in that day, and leap for joy, for behold, your reward is great in heaven..."[128] James gives further explanation, "Blessed is the man who remains steadfast under trial, for when he has stood the test he will receive the crown of life, which God has promised to those who love him."[129] A firm stance in the values that come from heaven will bring about the rewards of heaven.

When we consider the blessing of persecution we need to be careful to define the acceptable reason for persecution. Some professing Christians are accused of hypocrisy because they are hypocrites. Others are accused of being judgmental because they are, they do not base their standards or ideals on

128 Luke 6:22, 23

129 James 1:12

God's Word, but on their own opinions and preferences. The persecuted to whom Jesus referred are those who face trials because of the name for which they stand – Jesus Christ. If our persecution is not for the sake of the work of Jesus Christ in the establishment of God's counter-culture it is meaningless.

It is not you and I, but the righteousness that God establishes in our lives that offends the culture. Have you ever seen anyone get mad because a husband or wife, or their children got saved? The lives of those who are saved are transformed by God and it upsets those who want to cling to the sinful things of the world. Jesus explained that the accusations that come on account of our righteousness must be false if we are to be blessed. "Blessed are you when others revile you and persecute you and utter all kinds of evil against you falsely on my account." When we face the accusations of the world we must stand firm in righteousness so that they have no reason to accuse us. This is what is pleasing to God, and what will give us the blessing that Jesus pronounced upon the persecuted.

When we live under the blessing of God in His kingdom culture we realize that the trials we face here are only temporary. We face difficulties in this life as the world tries to drag us down, but God will sustain us through any trial and every tribulation if we will submit ourselves to Him. If we live the values of God's kingdom, we hold the eternal so dear that we realize there will come a day when we enter the dwelling place of God and the persecution of this life will become a fading, distant memory in the light of the City of God. "For this light momentary affliction is preparing for us an eternal weight of glory beyond all comparison, as we look not to the things that are seen but to the things that are unseen. For the things that are seen are transient, but the things that are unseen are eternal."[130]

The world around us lives according to a different culture, and values different things than the children of God. We are so often willing to compromise our conviction and values to accommodate a worldly society. We allow ourselves to be pushed into accepting and condoning things that Scripture teaches are wrong. Jesus made no pretense about the way the world would feel about us, and the way we live. If we are to live for God persecution will come, but it is when we stand firm in the face of difficulties and trial; when we are anchored in God's word, and when we hold the values of heaven with an uncompromising passion that Jesus cries out to us, "Blessed are you..." It is in the face of those things that we can make the claim that the kingdom of God has become our inheritance.

---

130 1 Corinthians 4:17, 18

The Great Counter Culture

W ebster's dictionary defines *counter culture* as *mores contrary to the accepted mores of the time and place.* This defines the call that God has extended to us through Jesus Christ, to be a counter culture in the world today. The church of this day has been struggling for decades to find an identity, and to find her place in the world. The place to which God has called the church may not be the place we are looking for, or the one we had hoped for; but the place to which He has called us is His kingdom. God desires to invade this world through His people, the culture they live, and the values they hold.

In Matthew 16:18 Jesus said, "on this rock I will build my church, and the gates of hell shall not prevail against it." For too many years we have mistaken what this verse means. In ancient days cities would surround themselves with walls and gates for their protection. Consider the implication of this: No city ever carried its gates off to war with them, in fact, the notion is ludicrous. But we think this verse means that the church can hide and will never be overcome by the world. That is not at all what it means! Jesus was telling us that the church was intended to be an offensive force waging war against the powers of hell; a force that carries the culture of God into a world that opposes the Christian lifestyle and culture.

The church has conformed to the culture of the world, and even embraced this culture for generations now. If the church is ever to see God move in power through her ranks again, it will be when we see a revival of the culture that Jesus came to establish. When He prayed, "Your kingdom come, your will be done, on earth as it is in heaven,"[131] He was praying for the culture of God to come from heaven, where it was, to earth, where it's needed. That is the call that God puts forth to us today.

Scripture speaks to us of a blessed life that comes with living this culture, yet we see so little of it. When we talk about, and pray for, revival we are asking God to once again establish His culture among His people. The Sermon on the Mount, and especially the beatitudes, are the manifesto of God's kingdom, and the definitive statement of His culture. We long for the days when God's Spirit moves in power through the church; this is the culture and these are the values through which He will move. It is when we see these values restored among God's people that we will see an awakening and a renewal of God's church.

---

131 Matthew 6:10

CPSIA information can be obtained at www.ICGtesting.com
Printed in the USA
BVOW041918110213

312936BV00002B/6/P

9 781449 782795